T0002183

POWER
POSITIVITY

I AM
FEARLESS

Hardie Grant

BOOKS

I HAVE A LOT OF THINGS
TO PROVE TO MYSELF.
ONE IS THAT I CAN LIVE
MY LIFE FEARLESSLY.

Oprah Winfrey

I'M NOT A GOOD TERRIFIED PERSON.
I LEARNED THAT A LONG TIME AGO.
YOU KNOW WHEN YOU WALK INTO
YOUR HOUSE AND THERE'S NOBODY
THERE AND ALL THE LIGHTS ARE
OUT, IT'S LIKE I JUST FEARLESSLY
GO INTO THE DARK, BECAUSE I KNOW
IF I START CREEPIN' OUT THAT IT'LL
GET ME. SO, I JUST TRY NOT TO
EVER BE AFRAID OF ANYTHING.

Stevie Nicks

YOU'VE GOT TO KNOW HOW
TO RESET AFTER FAILURE,
DISAPPOINTMENT AND
SETBACKS. YOU GOTTA LEARN
HOW TO GET BACK UP WHEN
YOU FALL, 'CAUSE THAT'S
PART OF BEING BRAVE.

Brené Brown

JUST DO *ANYTHING* – ANYTHING WILL LEAD TO SOMETHING ELSE AND YOU'VE JUST GOT TO GET OUT THERE AND TAKE A CHANCE.

Margot Robbie

MAYBE THE THING YOU'RE MOST SCARED OF IS EXACTLY WHAT YOU SHOULD DO.

Chris Evans

IF YOU'RE GONNA FAIL, FAIL BIG. I'M NOT A FALLBACK MENTALITY KIND OF PERSON. I DON'T WANT TO FALL BACK ON ANYTHING – IF I FALL, I'M GONNA FALL FORWARD!

Denzel Washington

KEEP PUSHING, FORGET THE FEAR, FORGET THE DOUBT. KEEP INVESTING AND KEEP BETTING ON YOURSELF.

Beyoncé

THERE IS NO TERROR IN A BANG, ONLY IN THE ANTICIPATION OF IT.

Alfred Hitchcock

YOU NEED TO CONSTANTLY STRETCH YOURSELF, TRAVEL, MEET NEW PEOPLE, ENGAGE IN NEW EXPERIENCES FEARLESSLY.

LaKeith Stanfield

ALWAYS GO A LITTLE FURTHER
INTO THE WATER THAN YOU
FEEL YOU ARE CAPABLE OF
BEING IN. GO A LITTLE BIT OUT
OF YOUR DEPTH. AND WHEN
YOU DON'T FEEL THAT YOUR
FEET ARE QUITE TOUCHING
THE BOTTOM, YOU'RE JUST
ABOUT IN THE RIGHT PLACE
TO DO SOMETHING EXCITING.

David Bowie

FEARLESS IS GETTING BACK UP
AND FIGHTING FOR WHAT YOU
WANT OVER AND OVER AGAIN ...
EVEN THOUGH EVERY TIME
YOU'VE TRIED BEFORE, YOU'VE
LOST. IT'S FEARLESS TO HAVE
FAITH THAT SOMEDAY THINGS
WILL CHANGE.

Taylor Swift

WE MUST TRAVEL IN THE DIRECTION OF OUR FEAR.

John Berryman

NOTHING IN LIFE IS TO BE FEARED, IT IS ONLY TO BE UNDERSTOOD.

Marie Curie

TO FEAR LOVE IS TO FEAR LIFE.

Bertrand Russell

I WILL FIGHT FOR WHAT I BELIEVE IN UNTIL I DROP DEAD. AND THAT'S WHAT KEEPS YOU ALIVE.

Barbara Castle

IF I CHOOSE NOT TO SPEAK
OUT OF FEAR THEN THERE'S
NO ONE THAT MY SILENCE IS
STANDING FOR. AND SO I CAME
TO REALISE THAT I CANNOT
STAND STANDING TO THE SIDE,
STANDING SILENT, I MUST FIND
THE STRENGTH TO SPEAK.

Amanda Gorman

EVERYTHING WORTH DOING
IN LIFE HAS RISK ... IT'S WORTH
ASKING YOURSELF "WHAT
RISKS ARE WORTH TAKING?"
AND ONCE YOU'VE DECIDED
TO TAKE THEM, THEN CHANGE
WHO YOU ARE SO THAT YOU
CAN WIN, YOU CAN DEFEAT,
YOU CAN MASTER THAT
THING AND OPEN A DOOR FOR
YOURSELF THAT OTHERWISE
WAS JUST SHUT.

Commander Chris Hadfield

WE MUST BE THE CHANGE WE WISH TO SEE IN THE WORLD.

Mahatma Gandhi

**STAND UP
AND SPEAK OUT.
YOUR STRONGEST
BELIEFS WILL HELP
YOU BECOME
FEARLESS.**

THE BEST WAY OUT IS ALWAYS THROUGH.

Robert Frost

DO SOMETHING THAT SCARES YOU AND THAT, INEVITABLY, WILL TEACH YOU TO BE FEARLESS.

Priyanka Chopra Jonas

IT IS BETTER TO DIE ON YOUR FEET THAN TO LIVE ON YOUR KNEES.

Dolores Ibárruri

LIFE IS EITHER A DARING ADVENTURE OR NOTHING.

Helen Keller

DREAM AS IF YOU'LL LIVE FOREVER.

LIVE AS IF YOU'LL DIE TODAY.

James Dean

LIFE MUST BE UNDERSTOOD BACKWARDS BUT ... IT MUST BE LIVED FORWARDS.

Søren Kierkegaard

**LIFE IS NOT MEANT
TO BE EASY, MY CHILD;
BUT TAKE COURAGE:
IT CAN BE DELIGHTFUL.**

George Bernard Shaw

I DO THINGS DIFFERENTLY,
BECAUSE I DON'T GO BY A RULE
BOOK, BECAUSE I LEAD FROM
THE HEART AND NOT THE HEAD.
AND ALBEIT THAT'S GOTTEN
ME INTO TROUBLE IN MY WORK,
BUT SOMEONE'S GOT TO GO
OUT THERE AND LOVE PEOPLE.

Diana, Princess of Wales

IT'S BETTER TO SPEAK OUT,
TO HAVE THAT MOMENT WHEN
YOU SAY, "I'M GOING TO DO
SOMETHING FOR MY SIDE."
AND THAT NEEDS A BIT OF
COURAGE. OUR COURAGE WAS
STRONGER THAN OUR FEAR.

Malala Yousafzai

THE SECRET TO REAPING THE GREATEST FRUITFULNESS AND THE GREATEST ENJOYMENT OF LIFE IS TO *LIVE DANGEROUSLY!*

Friedrich Nietzsche

WE KNOW WHAT
HAPPENS TO PEOPLE
WHO STAY IN THE
MIDDLE OF THE ROAD.
THEY GET RUN DOWN.

Aneurin Bevan

IT IS NOT THE STRENGTH
OF THE BODY THAT COUNTS,
BUT THE STRENGTH
OF THE SPIRIT.

J.R.R. Tolkien

HAVE NO FEAR OF PERFECTION; YOU'LL NEVER REACH IT.

Marie Curie

GO WITH YOUR GUT.

Bradley Cooper

DON'T EVER MAKE DECISIONS BASED ON FEAR. MAKE DECISIONS BASED ON HOPE AND POSSIBILITY. MAKE DECISIONS BASED ON WHAT SHOULD HAPPEN, NOT WHAT SHOULDN'T.

Michelle Obama

SOCIAL CHANGE IS BROUGHT ABOUT BY THOSE WHO DARE AND ACT.

Indira Gandhi

DO WHAT YOU FEEL IN YOUR HEART TO BE RIGHT – FOR YOU'LL BE CRITICISED ANYWAY.

Eleanor Roosevelt

ANYTIME YOU'RE PUTTING BARRIERS UP IN YOUR OWN LIFE, YOU'RE JUST LIMITING YOURSELF.

Harry Styles

TECHNIQUE AND ABILITY ALONE DO NOT GET YOU TO THE TOP; IT IS THE WILLPOWER THAT IS MOST IMPORTANT.

Junko Tabei

WHEN I GET REALLY, REALLY ANXIOUS BEFORE A SHOW, I JUST GO HARDER AND HARDER AND HARDER WHEN I'M PERFORMING.

Lizzo

WE HAVE TO FEAR IS FEAR ITSELF.

Franklin D. Roosevelt

DO NOT STOP THINKING OF LIFE AS AN ADVENTURE. YOU HAVE NO SECURITY UNLESS YOU CAN LIVE BRAVELY, EXCITINGLY, IMAGINATIVELY; UNLESS YOU CAN CHOOSE A CHALLENGE INSTEAD OF COMPETENCE.

Eleanor Roosevelt

I'VE BEEN ABSOLUTELY TERRIFIED EVERY MOMENT OF MY LIFE – AND I'VE NEVER LET IT KEEP ME FROM DOING A SINGLE THING I WANTED TO DO.

Georgia O' Keeffe

EVERY MOMENT WASTED
LOOKING BACK, KEEPS US
FROM MOVING FORWARD ...
IN THIS WORLD AND THE
WORLD OF TOMORROW,
WE MUST GO FORWARD
TOGETHER OR NOT AT ALL.

Hillary Clinton

WHAT'S WONDERFUL ABOUT
THE MET [BALL] AND THE
OPENING NIGHT IS THAT
PEOPLE FEEL VERY FEARLESS.
AND I THINK THAT GIVES
THEM LICENSE TO DRESS
IN A WAY THAT THEY MIGHT
NOT NORMALLY.

Anna Wintour

THEY'LL TELL YOU YOU'RE TOO LOUD, THAT YOU NEED TO WAIT YOUR TURN AND ASK THE RIGHT PEOPLE FOR PERMISSION. DO IT ANYWAY.

Alexandria Ocasio-Cortez

**YOU HAVE ENEMIES?
GOOD. THAT MEANS YOU'VE
STOOD UP FOR SOMETHING,
SOMETIME IN YOUR LIFE.**

I LOVE TO SEE A YOUNG
GIRL GO OUT AND GRAB
THE WORLD BY THE LAPELS.
LIFE'S A BITCH. YOU'VE GOT
TO GO OUT AND KICK ASS.

Maya Angelou

MY DESIRE TO SUCCEED
HAS ALWAYS BEEN GREATER
THAN MY FEAR. I'VE BEEN
SCARED TO DEATH ABOUT
A LOT OF THINGS, BUT THEN
I THINK, "OKAY, YOU GOTTA
BUCKLE UP, GIRL. YOU'VE GOT
YOURSELF HERE, SO GET OUT
THERE AND JUST DO IT."

Dolly Parton

TO BE FEARLESS, FOLLOW YOUR INSTINCTS. YOU ALREADY KNOW WHAT'S RIGHT; YOU JUST NEED TO LISTEN TO YOURSELF.

A HERO IS NO BRAVER
THAN AN ORDINARY PERSON,
BUT THEY ARE BRAVE
FIVE MINUTES LONGER.

ONE HAD BETTER DIE
FIGHTING AGAINST INJUSTICE
THAN DIE LIKE A DOG
OR A RAT IN A TRAP.

Ida B. Wells

GO TO THE EDGE OF THE CLIFF AND JUMP OFF. BUILD YOUR WINGS ON THE WAY DOWN.

Ray Bradbury

I HAVE LEARNED OVER THE YEARS THAT WHEN ONE'S MIND IS MADE UP, THIS DIMINISHES FEAR; KNOWING WHAT MUST BE DONE DOES AWAY WITH FEAR

I DON'T FEAR BEING OUTSPOKEN. THE ONLY THING I FEAR IS LOSING MY SENSE OF INTEGRITY OR LOSING SIGHT OF THE VALUES ON WHICH I GUIDE MY LIFE.

Constance Wu

A CRAZY THING HAPPENED –
THE VERY ACT OF DOING THE THING
THAT SCARED ME UNDID THE FEAR.
IT'S AMAZING THE POWER OF ONE
WORD. "YES" CHANGED MY LIFE.
"YES" CHANGED ME ...

CONTINUE TO DEFINE YOUR UNIQUE PATH IN FAITH AND WITH THE EXPERIENCE OF THE ACCOMPLISHED ADVENTURER THAT YOU ARE. YOU AND YOU ALONE ARE THE ONLY PERSON WHO CAN LIVE THE LIFE THAT WRITES THE STORY THAT YOU WERE MEANT TO TELL.

Kerry Washington

OUR EXISTENCE IS AN AMALGAMATION OF EVERY TRIUMPH, EVERY HARD-WON BATTLE, EVERY WOMAN WHO HAD AN IDEA AND MASSAGED IT, AND HAD THE COURAGE TO USE IT TO CHANGE THE WORLD.

Viola Davis

**ALL DOUBT
IS COWARDICE –
ALL TRUST IS BRAVE.**

Edward Bulwer-Lytton

**COURAGE IS ALMOST
A CONTRADICTION IN TERMS.
IT MEANS A STRONG DESIRE
TO LIVE TAKING THE FORM
OF A READINESS TO DIE.**

G.K. Chesterton

IF WE WANT TO CHANGE THE WORLD, WE HAVE TO DO IT OURSELVES AND I THINK WE ARE, AND I THINK WE WILL.

Blake Lively

EITHER LIFE ENTAILS COURAGE, OR IT CEASES TO BE LIFE.

E.M. Forster

COURAGE IS CONTAGIOUS. WHEN YOU FREE YOURSELF FROM FEAR, YOU SPREAD FEARLESSNESS TO OTHERS.

COWARDS DIE MANY TIMES BEFORE THEIR DEATHS; THE VALIANT NEVER TASTE OF DEATH BUT ONCE.

William Shakespeare

SOMETIMES YOU'RE A LITTLE BIT SCARED, BUT MOST OF THE TIME ... YOU'RE REALLY JUST EXCITED ABOUT IT. SO YOU JUST KIND OF THROW FEAR OUT OF THE WAY.

Simone Biles

WHAT REALLY COUNTS IS
NOT THE IMMEDIATE ACT OF
COURAGE OR OF VALOUR, BUT
THOSE WHO BEAR THE STRUGGLE
DAY IN AND DAY OUT – NOT THE
SUNSHINE PATRIOTS BUT THOSE
WHO ARE WILLING TO STAND
FOR A LONG PERIOD OF TIME.

John F. Kennedy

THE BEST THING THAT ARTISTS
AND PEOPLE THAT ARE BORN
A LITTLE BIT DIFFERENT,
BORN WITH A LITTLE EXTRA
CREATIVITY, A LITTLE EXTRA
ANXIETY, A LITTLE EXTRA
SOMETHING ... IS OUR WILD
THINKING OUR RECKLESS
BEHAVIOUR, OUR ABILITY
TO BE FEARLESS.

Lady Gaga

IF YOU NEVER FELT
SCARED, YOU'D NEVER
GET TO FEEL BRAVE.

FEARLESS PEOPLE OFTEN FACED THE HARDEST CHALLENGES. NOW THEY KNOW WHAT TO DO.

IF YOU CAN DANCE AND BE FREE AND NOT BE EMBARRASSED, YOU CAN RULE THE WORLD.

Amy Poehler

NOTHING IS TERRIBLE EXCEPT FEAR ITSELF.

Francis Bacon

THE MOST COURAGEOUS ACT IS STILL TO THINK FOR YOURSELF. ALOUD.

Coco Chanel

YOU ONLY LIVE ONCE, BUT IF YOU DO IT RIGHT, ONCE IS ENOUGH.

Mae West

DO ONE THING EVERY DAY THAT SCARES YOU.

Mary Schmich

YOU MUST DO THE THING YOU THINK YOU CANNOT DO.

Eleanor Roosevelt

A LOT OF PEOPLE ARE AFRAID
TO SAY WHAT THEY WANT.
THAT'S WHY THEY DON'T
GET WHAT THEY WANT.

Madonna

YOU CAN'T SEE WHAT IS AROUND THE CORNER, BUT YOU HAVE TO KEEP GOING FORWARD ANYWAY.

REAL COURAGE IS NOT GRACE UNDER PRESSURE. IT'S DOING THE RIGHT THING WHEN IT'S FRIGHTENING AND HURTS.

Ramsey Clark

DON'T LET IMAGINARY FEARS GET THE BEST OF YOU. YOU HAVE ENOUGH REAL BATTLES TO FIGHT.

**FEAR DEFEATS MORE
PEOPLE THAN ANY OTHER
ONE THING IN THE WORLD.**

OVER FEAR.

Janelle Monáe

YOU CAN'T LAUGH AND BE AFRAID AT THE SAME TIME – OF ANYTHING. IF YOU'RE LAUGHING, I DEFY YOU TO BE AFRAID.

Stephen Colbert

**COURAGE CALLS
TO COURAGE
EVERYWHERE.**

Millicent Fawcett

BE NOT AFRAID OF LIFE. BELIEVE THAT LIFE *IS* WORTH LIVING, AND YOUR BELIEF WILL HELP CREATE THE FACT.

William James

**EVEN THE FEAR OF DEATH
IS NOTHING COMPARED TO
THE FEAR OF NOT HAVING LIVED
AUTHENTICALLY AND FULLY.**

Frances Moore Lappé

THERE ARE FEW THINGS MORE LIBERATING IN THIS LIFE THAN HAVING YOUR WORST FEAR REALISED.

Conan O'Brien

I WILL GO WHERE THERE IS NO PATH, AND I WILL LEAVE A TRAIL.

Muriel Strode

I'M LEARNING TO WORRY
LESS ABOUT WHAT PEOPLE
THINK, AND NOT TO BE
AFRAID TO SAY THE TRUTH.

Elliot Page

YOU'RE WORRYING ABOUT THINGS GOING WRONG, BUT WHAT IF THEY WENT RIGHT?

WHEN YOU ATTEMPT SOMETHING NEW, THERE'S ALWAYS FEAR.

Gloria Steinem

YOU HAVE TO LIVE WITHOUT THE FEAR OF MAKING A FOOL OUT OF YOURSELF OR DREAMING BIG.

Sofía Vergara

I HAVE COME TO
UNDERSTAND AND
LISTEN TO THE FEAR.
I WALK TOWARD IT
AND I LEAN INTO IT
TO FIND INFORMATION –
AND THINGS THAT IT
HAS TO TEACH ME.

Tracee Ellis Ross

LETTING GO OF FEAR WILL MAKE YOU FREE – TO BE CREATIVE, TO BE HAPPY, TO FOLLOW YOUR DREAMS.

Bruce Lee

Published in 2023 by
Hardie Grant Books, an imprint
of Hardie Grant Publishing

Hardie Grant Books (London)
5th & 6th Floors
52–54 Southwark Street
London SE1 1UN

Hardie Grant Books (Melbourne)
Building 1, 658 Church Street
Richmond, Victoria 3121

hardiegrantbooks.com

British Library Cataloguing-in-
Publication Data. A catalogue
record for this book is available
from the British Library.

I AM FEARLESS
by Hardie Grant Books

ISBN: 9781784886271

Publishing Director: Kajal Mistry
Acting Publishing Director:
Emma Hopkin
Commissioning Editor: Kate Burkett
Text curated by: Satu Fox
Editorial Assistant: Harriet Thornley
Design: Claire Warner Studio

Colour Reproduction by p2d
Printed and bound in China by
Leo Paper Products Ltd.